W9-CAL-567

NOTE TO PARENTS

Welcome to Kingfisher Readers! This program is designed to help young readers build skills, confidence, and a love of reading as they explore their favorite topics.

These tips can help you get more from the experience of reading books together. But remember, the most important thing is to make reading fun!

Tips to Warm Up Before Reading

- Look through the book with your child. Ask them what they notice about the pictures.
- Wonder aloud together. Ask questions and make predictions. What will this book be about? What are some words we could expect to find on these pages?

While Reading

- Take turns or read together until your child takes over.
- Point to the words as you say them.
- When your child gets stuck on a word, ask if the picture could help. Then think about the first letter too.
- Accept and praise your child's contributions.

After Reading

- Look back at the things your child found interesting. Encourage connections to other things you both know.
- Draw pictures or make models to explore these ideas.
- Read the book again soon, to build fluency.

With five distinct levels and a wealth of appealing topics, the Kingfisher Readers series provides children with an exciting way to learn to read about the world around them. Enjoy!

Ellie Costa, M.S. Ed.
Literacy Specialist, Bank Street School for Children, New York

KINGFISHER
READERS

level
3

Firefighters

Chris Oxlade and Thea Feldman

KINGFISHER
NEW YORK

KINGFISHER
LONDON & NEW YORK

Copyright © Kingfisher 2014
Published in the United States by Kingfisher.
175 Fifth Ave., New York, NY 10010
Kingfisher is an imprint of Macmillan Children's Books, London.
All rights reserved.

Series editor: Thea Feldman
Literacy consultant: Ellie Costa, Bank Street College, New York

ISBN: 978-0-7534-7122-7 (HB)
ISBN: 978-0-7534-7123-4 (PB)

Kingfisher books are available for special promotions and
premiums. For details contact: Special Markets Department,
Macmillan, 175 Fifth Ave., New York, NY 10010.

For more information, please visit
www.kingfisherbooks.com

Printed in China
9 8 7 6 5 4 3 2 1
1TR/1013/WKT/UG/105MA

Picture credits
The Publisher would like to thank the following for permission to reproduce their material.
Every care has been taken to trace copyright holders. However, if there have been
unintentional omissions or failure to trace copyright holders, we apologize and will,
if informed, endeavor to make corrections in any future edition.
Top = t; Bottom = b; Center = c; Left = l; Right = r
Cover Shutterstock/Mike Brake and pages 3t Shutterstock/Monkey Business Images;
3tc Shutterstock/Zulhazmi Zabri; 3c Shutterstock/Pavel Bortel; 3cb Shutterstock/Will
Thomson; 3b Shutterstock/Keith Muratori; 45 Shutterstock/Ronald Caswell; 6 Shutterstock/
Monkey Business Images; 7t Getty/Riser; 7b Corbis/Creasource; 8 Shutterstock/mikeledray;
9 Shutterstock/Zulhazmi Zabri; 10 Shutterstock/Monkey Business Images; 11 Shutterstock/
Bryan Eastham; 12 Shutterstock/Jerry Sharp; 14 Shutterstock; 15 Alamy/Alex Ramsay;
16 Shutterstock/Steve Noakes; 17t Shutterstock/TFoxFoto; 17b Shutterstock/Pavel Bortel;
18–19 Shutterstock/Jeff Krushinski; 18 Shutterstock/Keith Muratori; 19 Alamy/Jack Sullivan;
20 Alamy/Ian Marlow; 21t Corbis/Uwe Anspach; 21b Alamy/Sagaphoto; 22 Alamy/Michael
Routh; 23 Shutterstock/Will Thomson; 24 Alamy/Imagebroker; 25 Shutterstock/Gary Blakeley;
28 Shutterstock/Luis Louro; 29 Alamy/Shout; 31 Getty/Riser.

Contents

What is a firefighter?

A firefighter is someone who helps in an **emergency**. A firefighter's main job is to put out fires. When a fire starts, a team of firefighters rushes to the fire. The firefighters use hoses, ladders, and other **equipment** to put out the fire. They rescue people trapped by fire, too.

Firefighters help with other emergencies. They rescue people after accidents such as car crashes. They also help people trapped in floods or on cliffs by the sea.

Ready and waiting

Firefighters wait at the fire station until they are needed for an emergency. While they wait, they clean and repair their fire engines and other equipment. They also practice their firefighting skills.

When an emergency call comes in, the firefighters leap into action. They jump in their fire engines as fast as they can. The engines zoom out of the fire station.

They race toward the emergency. The drivers turn on flashing lights and loud **sirens** to warn people to get out of the way.

Firefighter fact
Some fire stations have a metal pole that firefighters slide down to get to their fire engines quickly.

Training to fight fires

Firefighters train for months before they are allowed to tackle fires. They learn how to work hoses, **pumps**, ladders, and all sorts of other equipment. They learn how fires start and how to put fires out. They also learn first aid and how to find people who have been trapped by fires.

Firefighters have to be brave and fit. They learn how to work in places where it is very hot and smoky. They also learn to be part of a firefighting team.

Firefighters train with real fires. Sometimes firefighters set fire to empty, old buildings. Then they fight the fire to practice using their equipment.

A firefighter learns to run through flames.

Special clothes

Firefighters wear tough jackets and pants as well as thick gloves when they tackle fires. The clothes are made from special materials that do not catch fire even if flames touch them. They are also waterproof.

Firefighters always wear helmets to protect their head. They wear waterproof boots, too.

When a firefighter goes into a building full of smoke, he or she wears a **breathing apparatus**. The apparatus is a mask connected to a tank of air. It helps the firefighter breathe.

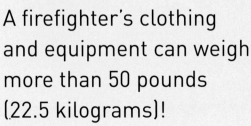

Firefighter fact
A firefighter's clothing and equipment can weigh more than 50 pounds (22.5 kilograms)!

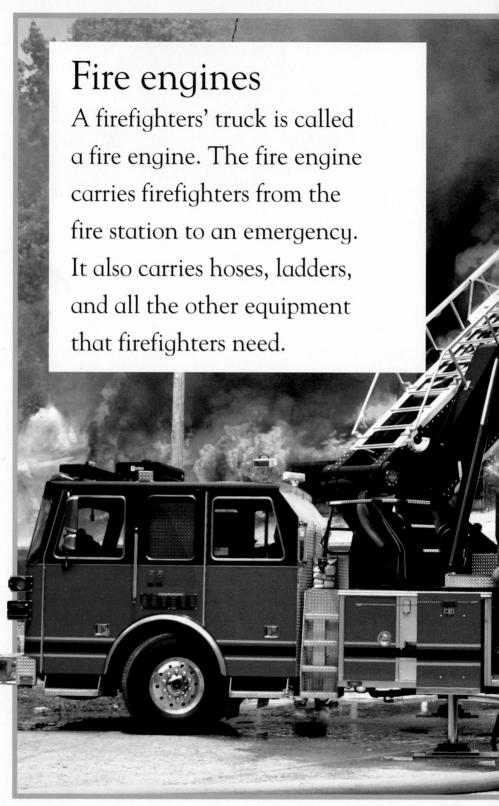

Fire engines

A firefighters' truck is called a fire engine. The fire engine carries firefighters from the fire station to an emergency. It also carries hoses, ladders, and all the other equipment that firefighters need.

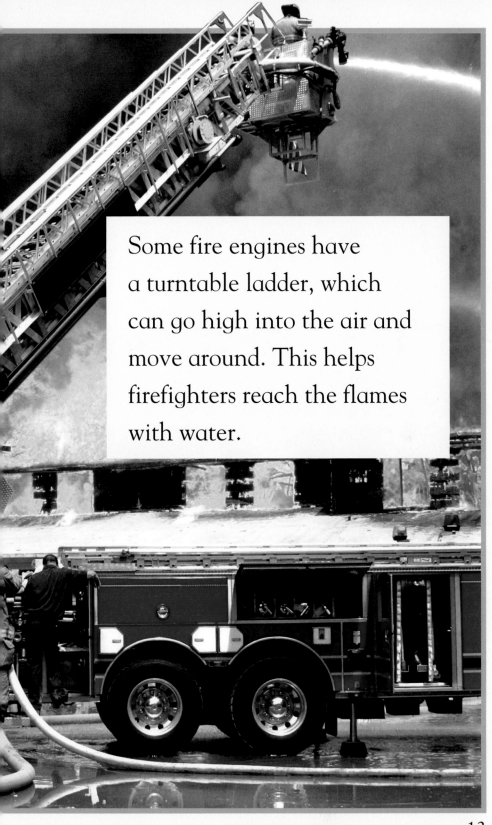

Some fire engines have a turntable ladder, which can go high into the air and move around. This helps firefighters reach the flames with water.

Making a plan

When firefighters arrive at an emergency, they jump out, ready for action. The head firefighter quickly makes a plan and tells the other firefighters what to do. Some firefighters unload the ladders.

Other firefighters unroll long hoses.
A hose connects to the fire engine's pump.

Where do firefighters get water? Sometimes their fire engine has a water tank inside it. In towns they can get water from **hydrants**. In the country they sometimes take water from rivers or ponds.

Opening a hydrant for water

Putting out flames

Firefighters pour water on fires to cool down the fire and put out the flames.

Water cannot put out burning oil or gas. The oil or gas will float on the water and keep burning. Firefighters put out oil or gas fires with **foam**.

Water comes out of a **nozzle** at the end of a hose. Firefighters have to hold the nozzle tightly. The force of the water rushing out of the hose can push them backward.

A firefighter sprays foam on burning tires.

Into the smoke

Sometimes firefighters have to go into buildings that are on fire. They go in buildings to put out flames or to rescue people who are trapped inside.

The rooms may be full of smoke. Smoke makes people cough and choke.

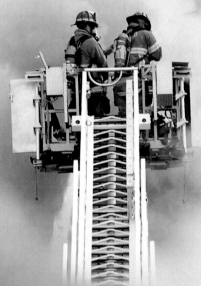

A firefighter wearing her breathing apparatus

Breathing equipment helps firefighters breathe in smoky places. It also protects them if the smoke is poisonous. Masks keep the smoke out of their eyes.

Smoke can make it hard to see. The smoke also makes it hard for firefighters to find people who may be trapped. They look through a special camera that helps them find people in the smoke.

A fireman uses a camera to search for people in smoke

Rescue!

Firefighters also help people in need of rescue. They take people to safe places.

Sometimes people get trapped in their cars after an accident. Firefighters use tools called **cutters** and **spreaders** to get them out. A cutter is like a giant pair of scissors. It slices through the tough metal of a car. A spreader pushes the metal apart.

Firefighters use boats to carry people away from flooded homes.

They use ropes to rescue people from rivers or from cliffs.

Fighting wildfires

Fires in forests are called **wildfires**. They can be hard to reach. Firefighters use off-road fire engines that can drive over rough ground. Sometimes specially trained firefighters wear parachutes and jump from planes to reach a wildfire.

Firefighters can use helicopters to drop water on a wildfire

Wildfires in forests spread quickly because trees in forests are close together. To try to stop a fire, firefighters cut down trees to make spaces between them.

Fighting a forest fire in California

Fire fact
On a windy day, a wildfire can burn through a forest faster than a person can run.

Special firefighting jobs

All airports have a team of firefighters and special fire engines. The team is always ready for action when aircraft are taking off and landing, in case there is an emergency.

Firefighter fact
Firefighting teams in airports practice their skills by setting fire to old aircraft.

An airport fire engine has a huge nozzle on top that sprays foam onto burning fuel.

Some firefighters work on special boats. These are like fire engines at sea. The firefighters put out fires in buildings along the shore. They also put out fires on ships and oil rigs.

A firefighting boat rushes to a fire.

Firefighters in the past

Hundreds of years ago firefighters used fire carts. They pulled the carts through the streets to reach a fire. Then they pumped water through the hoses by hand.

In some cities, people called fire wardens watched for fires from tall towers.

Most buildings were made of wood, which burns easily. Buildings were very close together, so flames could jump from one building to the next. If a fire grew too big, the firefighters could not put it out. Sometimes fires destroyed hundreds of houses.

Firefighter fact
The first firefighters worked in the city of Rome in Italy about 2,000 years ago.

There was a huge fire in London in 1666. Firefighters tore down buildings to try to stop the flames from spreading.

Fire safety

Most fires start by accident, such as when cooking oil catches fire or when electric wires break. Sometimes burning cigarettes start fires. Firefighters tell people how to prevent these kinds of accidents.

They also tell people to put up **smoke detectors**. They teach people how to use **fire extinguishers**. Firefighters visit homes, schools, offices, and factories to talk about fire safety.

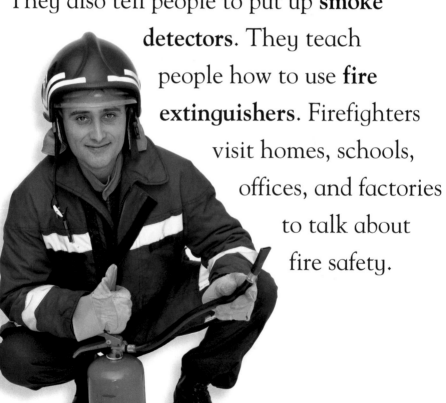

Glossary

breathing apparatus a mask connected to an air tank that firefighters use when they fight a smoky fire

cutter a machine that cuts through metal like a pair of powerful scissors

emergency when someone needs help quickly for safety or health reasons

equipment things people use to do their job, such as firefighters' hoses and pumps

fire extinguisher a container of water or foam that is used to put out a small fire

foam a collection of many tiny bubbles

hydrant a pipe in the street from which firefighters can get water for their hoses

nozzle the pointed end of a pipe

pump a machine that pushes water or foam through a pipe

siren a piece of equipment that makes a very loud whirring noise to warn people of danger

smoke detector a machine that makes a loud alarm noise when it senses smoke from a fire

spreader a machine that pushes apart pieces of metal. Firefighters use spreaders to help rescue people trapped in their cars after an accident

sprinkler a piece of equipment, which looks like a shower head, that is attached to the ceiling of a room. A sprinkler sprays water if a fire starts there

wildfire a fire in a forest or out in the country

winch equipment that helps lift heavy things

Index

If you have enjoyed reading
this book, look out for more in
the Kingfisher Readers series!

Collect
and read
them all!

KINGFISHER READERS: LEVEL 3

Ancient Rome ☐
Cars ☐
Creepy-Crawlies ☐
Dinosaur World ☐
Firefighters ☐
Record Breakers—The Biggest ☐
Volcanoes ☐

KINGFISHER READERS: LEVEL 4

The Arctic and Antarctica ☐
Flight ☐
Human Body ☐
Pirates ☐
Rivers ☐
Sharks ☐
Weather ☐

For a full list of Kingfisher Readers books, plus
guidance for teachers and parents and activities
and fun stuff for kids, go to the Kingfisher Readers
website: **www.kingfisherreaders.com**